GORILLAS:
The Real Story

by Chloe Garcia

Editorial Offices: Glenview, Illinois • Parsippany, New Jersey • New York, New York
Sales Offices: Needham, Massachusetts • Duluth, Georgia • Glenview, Illinois
Coppell, Texas • Sacramento, California • Mesa, Arizona

Gorillas have strong, muscular arms. Their arms are longer than their legs.

Gorillas: The Real Story

When you hear the word *gorilla,* do you think of a big, ferocious beast? Maybe you have seen movies in which gorillas pound their chests with their fists and roar angrily.

It is true that gorillas are big—they can weigh up to 600 pounds and stand up to 6 feet tall. They have powerful arms. They look like they can do harm.

But scientists who study gorillas tell a different story about them. They have learned that gorillas are usually shy and peaceful. They are also very intelligent. Let's learn the real story about gorillas.

---

ferocious: fierce

pound: hit

Mountain gorillas are the largest gorillas, with the longest hair. Their hair keeps them warm in the mountains.

Gorillas Are Not Monkeys

Many people think that gorillas are monkeys, but they are not. Monkeys are smaller and have tails. Gorillas belong to the family of animals called *great apes.*

Great apes include gorillas, chimpanzees (chim pan ZEES), and bonobos (buh NOH bohs). All these species are from Africa. Great apes also include orangutans (uh RANG uh tans), which are found on the Indonesian islands of Sumatra and Borneo.

Gorillas are the largest of the great apes. There are three kinds of gorillas: the western lowland gorilla, the eastern lowland gorilla, and the mountain gorilla.

Gorillas have big toes on their feet that work like the thumbs on their hands to help them grasp objects.

What Do Gorillas Look Like?

Gorillas have thick, wiry hair covering most of their bodies. The parts of a gorilla's body that do not have hair are the face, chest, fingers, palms, armpits, and soles of the feet. A gorilla's head is very large, with a forehead that bulges out. Gorillas have little ears and small brown eyes.

Gorillas have five fingers on each hand and five toes on each foot. They can grab things with both their hands and their feet.

Gorillas can stand on their legs, but they do not walk upright. They walk on their hands and feet. They keep the soles of their feet flat and the knuckles of their hands curled and on the ground.

---

soles: bottoms
upright: standing up

Gorillas Are Not Aggressive

Gorillas are not predators. They do not eat meat. Gorillas eat fruit, leaves, roots, and other plant material. They also eat insects and worms.

Gorillas may look big and scary, but usually they are not aggressive.

However, gorillas sometimes act in agressive ways when they are in danger. They stand up, stamp their feet, and pound the ground with the palms of their hands. They beat their chests and curl back their lips to show their teeth. They tear up and throw plants. They scream and charge.

But gorillas usually only do these things when they feel that they or their young are in danger. They are gentle creatures that live in families. They will give up their lives to defend their families.

Extend Language **Multiple-Meaning Words**

Some English words have more than one meaning. For example, the word *pound* can mean "hit." It is also a unit of measure.

What is the meaning of *stamp* on this page? Can you think of another meaning of *stamp*?

---

predators: animals that hunt and kill for food
charge: run to attack

A silverback in Virunga National Park, in the Democratic Republic of Congo

Gorilla Families

The leader of a gorilla family is an older male known as a *silverback*. This name refers to the hair color on its back. The silverback's hair turns gray because of age. This happens when the male gorilla is about 10 to 13 years old.

The silverback is the oldest male gorilla in the family. It is also the strongest and largest. The other members in a gorilla family are usually one or two younger males, a few females, and their young.

The silverback is the protector of the family. It also makes sure no other male gorillas try to become the leader of the family. When other male gorillas try to do this, the silverback acts aggressively to scare them away.

When it is four months old, a baby gorilla is strong enough to ride on its mother's back.

Gorillas are very gentle, affectionate, and patient with their young. If a young weaned gorilla loses its mother, adult male gorillas will care for it.

When young gorillas get too playful, adult gorillas will often make them behave with a stern look or grunt. Young gorillas learn from the adults how to look for food and how to make their nests to sleep in each night.

weaned: able to eat food other than its mother's milk

Gorillas use many facial expressions to communicate. This gorilla is communicating calm and contentment.

Gorilla Communication

Gorillas use their faces and bodies to communicate. They make faces, stare, cross their arms, or stamp their feet.

Gorillas also make about twenty-five distinct sounds. Baby gorillas make whimpering sounds that seem to mean "Mama! Where are you?" Older gorillas make a sound that may mean "What was that?" Comfortable gorillas will often grunt or purr, especially when they are eating a favorite food. Gorillas also chuckle, roar, growl, and scream.

Dr. Francine Patterson with Koko

Koko's Case

Koko is a female lowland gorilla born in 1971 in the San Francisco Zoo. When Koko was one year old, she became part of a research project conducted by Dr. Francine "Penny" Patterson. Dr. Patterson wanted to find out if gorillas could learn to communicate with humans. Gorillas cannot talk, but Dr. Patterson thought they might be able to learn signs to communicate.

Dr. Patterson started teaching Koko sign language. Dr. Patterson had to make a special gorilla sign language for Koko because gorilla's hands are different from human hands. Within a few years, Koko learned to make hundreds of signs. Later she seemed to know over 1,000 signs. She understood about 2,000 words of spoken English.

The area highlighted in purple in the map shows gorilla habitats in Africa.

Gorilla Habitats

The habitats of the three kinds of gorillas—western lowland gorillas, eastern lowland gorillas, and mountain gorillas—are in different parts of Africa. Each place is an environment.

Western lowland gorillas live in tropical rain forests in the Central African Republic, the Democratic Republic of Congo, Cameroon, Gabon, Equatorial Guinea, and Nigeria.

Eastern lowland gorillas live in tropical rain forests in the eastern Democratic Republic of Congo.

Mountain gorillas live in high altitude forests in Rwanda, Uganda, and eastern Democratic Republic of Congo.

---

habitats: places where plants and animals live

A western lowland gorilla at the San Francisco Zoo

Gorillas in Danger

Gorillas need a lot of space to look for the wild plants they use for food. This presents a problem because people want to use the land that gorillas need. Some people want to cut down trees and turn forests into farmland. This is not good for the gorillas. Some people also kill gorillas to sell gorilla meat.

These activities cause dangers for all three kinds of gorillas. There are about 100,000 western lowland gorillas left in the wild. These are the smallest kind of gorillas. Some are seen in zoos. There are fewer than 5,000 eastern lowland gorillas. Their population is dropping quickly because of human wars and loss of habitat. A few of these gorillas are in zoos.

But the smallest population of gorillas is that of the mountain gorillas. There are only about 700 of them left in the mountains of central Africa. There are none at all in zoos.

Dian Fossey lived among mountain gorillas in Africa for many years.

Helping Gorillas

Many people are working to help gorillas survive. One person who studied gorillas and tried to protect them was Dian Fossey, an American scientist.

In 1967, Dian went to Africa to study mountain gorillas. She spent almost 18 years living among the mountain gorillas in Rwanda, studying their lives. The gorillas seemed to trust and accept her.

One day, a gorilla that Dian liked very much was killed by a hunter. Dian was sad and angry. She started a foundation to help protect other gorillas.

Other conservation groups exist to protect gorillas and their habitats. These groups want gorillas to have a good chance to live in the forests and mountains of Africa.

How do you feel, or think, about gorillas in Africa?